DEVELOPING EKKLESIA

From Just "Doing Church" to Developing *Ekklesia* and Bringing in Kingdom

A Study Based on *Ekklesia* By Ed Silvoso

Dr. Ronald E. Cottle

DR. RONALD E. COTTLE

Developing Ekklesia

© 2021 by Dr. Ronald E. Cottle All rights reserved.

This book is protected under the copyright laws of the United States of America. This book may not be copied or reprinted for commercial gain or profit. The use of short quotations or occasional page copying for personal, or group study is permitted and encouraged. Permission will be granted upon request. Unless otherwise indicated, Scripture quotations are from the King James Version of the Bible.

REC Ministries
664 Sweetwater Drive
Cataula, GA 31804
www.roncottle.com

Unless otherwise noted, Scripture is taken from the New King James Version of the Bible, World Bible Publishers, Inc., Iowa City, IA.

Other translations quoted:

NIV — New International Version, Copyright © 1973, 1978, 1984 by International Bible Society, Zondervan Publishing House. Used by Permission

NKJV — New King James Version, Copyright © 1982, Thomas Nelson, Inc. Used by Permission

AMP — Scripture quotations taken from the AMPLIFIED BIBLE, Copyright © 1954, 1958, 1962, 1964, 1965, 1987 by The Lockman Foundation. Used by permission. (www.Lockman.org)

NLT — HOLY BIBLE, NEW LIVING TRANSLATION, Copyright © 1996 by Tyndale Charitable Trust.

TABLE OF CONTENTS

INTRODUCTION 4

CHAPTER 1 – FIRST CHALLENGE TO EXISTING PERCEPTIONS 8

CHAPTER 2 – SECOND CHALLENGE TO EXISTING PERCEPTIONS 14

CHAPTER 3 – COMPETENCE VS. COMMITMENT 19

ABOUT THE AUTHOR 27

THE COTTLE LIBRARY 31

DR. RONALD E. COTTLE

INTRODUCTION

This booklet is intended to be a broad sweep through the highlights of "*Ekklesial* History." **Jesus Christ, God the Son, was in the *side* of the Father**. He *created* Adam, the man. He *made* the cosmos, the heavens, and the earth. The Bible does not say that our Creator, Father, created Jesus, the Son. It does not say that He made the Son. When we first meet God in Scripture, He is a Trinity of Father, Son, and Holy Spirit, all one but not the same.

The Church Fathers captured this reality by saying that "the Son *proceeds* from the Father." This indicates oneness — one but not the same. Later they clarified this even further by saying: "They are of one *essentia* but three *persona*: one essence in three persons."

Eve was in the *side* of Adam. This indicates oneness — *one* but not the *same*. She came from his side to indicate oneness but not sameness. She did not come from his head to indicate superiority nor from his feet to indicate inferiority.

> 7 For this reason a man shall leave his father and mother and be joined to his wife, 8 and the two shall become one flesh; so then they are no longer two, but one flesh (Mark 10:7-8).

The Church was in the *side* of Christ. This indicates oneness but not sameness. On the cross, they pierced His heart and out came blood and water. The result was redemption and cleansing, pardon and purity, and new birth by the blood and new life by the Spirit. This is the essence and the message of the Church and its Gospel, it's Good News. She is one with Christ but not the same!

The *Ekklesia* is in the *side* of the Church. This indicates oneness but not sameness. Were it not for the Church there could be no *Ekklesia*. Do not despise the Church; she is the mother of the *Ekklesia*, its womb and human source. The best of the Church will survive in the *Ekklesia*, but those elements that are not of "the blood and the water" will not.

Without the Father there would be no Son; without Adam there would be no Eve; without the Son there would be no Church; without the Church there would be no Ekklesia; and without the Ekklesia there can be no Kingdom.

In this booklet we will discuss various paradigm shifts in Church history, and how they arrived with transitions to existing ways of thinking about the Church. We will discover that we are in the beginning of another great transition. We must now consider how we can understand these transitions and the relationship between the *Ekklesia* and the already kingdom of God on the earth.

CHAPTER 1 - FIRST CHALLENGE TO EXISTING PERCEPTIONS

Every major mega-paradigm transition in history came with challenges to existing perceptions. The first of these challenges we will consider is this one:

> It is the responsibility and challenge of those with a new revelation to process it constructively so that they apply it without destroying, damaging, or dishonoring what is already in place (Silvoso, p. 236).

In other words, those of us who have the revelation of the Ekklesia must find what has been missing in the modern expression of the Church to add the new revelation to what is already in place and make it complete. To those of us who have the revelation of the Ekklesia, this must be our *modus operandi*, our mindset. Jesus said in Matthew 13:33b, "The kingdom of heaven is like leaven, which a woman took and hid in three measures of meal till it was all leavened," showing us that this will take some time.

And it was Jesus Who taught us the principle of introducing new truth in Matthew 9:16: "No one puts a piece of unshrunk cloth on an old garment; for the patch pulls away from the garment, and the tear is made worse."

This is what Jesus is saying, that the new must age and mature before it can be of any good to the old. Jesus re-emphasized this principle in the next verse. Matthew 9:17 says,

> "Nor do they put new (*kianos*-renewed) wine into old wineskins, or else the wineskins break, the wine is spilled, and the wineskins are ruined. But they put new wine into new wineskins, and both are preserved."

The *rhema* word here is this: Both the old and the new are important and are to be preserved together. The old garment and the new garment are of value to God. The old wine and the new wine. Both the old garment and the new piece (patch) have intrinsic value; you do not want to sacrifice the one for the other! The new must age and mature before it can be of any good to the old. It cannot complete or benefit the old if it's inevitable development (shrinkage) will tear it away from the old.

It is all too common to see people with a new revelation calling it "better" and going about breaking the bottles of the old, vintage wine! The older the wine, the "better" it is to human taste; that is why it is so expensive. This principle is so important that it appears in all three Synoptic Gospels, Matthew 9, Mark 2, and Luke 5. Dr. Luke, one who could probably afford the best wine and certainly understood the principle, added this verse in his account. "And no one, having drunk old wine, immediately desires new; for he says, 'The old (*palaios—* aged) is better (*chrestos—*good, gentle, not harsh or bitter, kind, comfortable)'" (Luke 5:39). We must honor and affirm the old wine, the traditional Church, while lifting the revelation and power of the new wine, the revelation of Ekklesia. Let us keep strife and "superiority" out of this transition. Contention will only weaken both.

Our first challenge, then, is this: We must introduce our revelation without an air of "superiority," anger, or dishonor to the Church which brought us into Christ. Consider a relay race. It is not the runner but the baton in the runner's hand that wins the race. This is our responsibility, not the Church's. We have the new revelation of the Ekklesia, we must introduce and plant that revelation into the church with care and love.

CHAPTER 2 – SECOND CHALLENGE TO EXISTING PERCEPTIONS

I said above that there are two challenges to the existing perceptions of paradigm transitions in Church history. The first is that we must not fail to honor the tradition of the existing paradigm as we make the shift to the new. The second challenge we face is that of "cohesiveness versus inclusiveness." When a powerful new revelation like the *Ekklesia* is discovered, the natural response is to go as wide as possible to get others involved as soon as possible. This is a mistake! We must go *deep* before we go *wide*.

Silvoso proposes his 5 – 15 – 80% principle to resolve this challenge. In these early years of this paradigm shift, we must focus on strengthening the *Ekklesia* more than on broadening it.

Five percent of the men and women involved are the *Visionaries*, immediate adopters, champions, eager for something better.

Fifteen percent are the *Implementers* – early adopters, readily convinced, open to the future.

However, eighty percent are the *Maintainers* – late adopters, those who need to see it work before embracing it, those reluctant to change.

And right here is a very important principle: We must not despise the Maintainers! They are valuable to the *Ekklesia*. They take care of and maintain the wheels of ministry day in and day out. They are faithful about maintaining what is already in place, and we would be lost without them. Indeed, without them we will never win, but always remain a scab on the Body of Christ, a loud minority without the power to effect meaningful and lasting change. The wise strategy, then, is to focus on the five percent and encourage the fifteen percent to keep the revelation pure and clear. Then, after these are reasonably established and stable in their commitment, we exercise patience while the eighty percenters, the Maintainers of the old system, observe and *ultimately* embrace the new. Examples of this are: the early Church, early Methodism, Pentecostals, and Charismatics. All of these presented new paradigms, but it took more than one generation.

Our purpose in this season is to consider the experience of Christ in us and through us by His Holy Spirit, and the current paradigm shift into the age of the *Ekklesia*. This could very well be the final substage of the Church Age begun at the Great Commissioning of the Apostles, the ascension of Christ, and the day of Pentecost. The time for fulfillment seems to be upon us. In the next brief chapter, we will consider an important principle for expansion on this strategy.

CHAPTER 3 – COMPETENCE VS. COMMITMENT

Let us now expand on this strategy of paradigm shift by understanding the principle of competence versus commitment. This principle is tricky. I have seen this alone defeat some competent, charismatic leaders. It would be wonderful if our core group, the center of gravity, the five percent, were made up of the most competent people available. However, that is seldom the case. The rule is: Competent leaders attract committed people who at first are not necessarily the most competent ones. One thinks of Jesus and His twelve disciples.

But unlike Christ, this has sometimes discouraged and even paralyzed some leaders. We must learn to "work with those whom the Lord provides." 1 Samuel 22:1-2 tells us that,

> 1 David therefore departed from there and escaped to the cave of Adullam. So when his brothers and all his father's house heard it, they went down there to him. 2 And everyone who was in distress, everyone who was in debt, and everyone who was

discontented gathered to him. So he became captain over them. And there were about four hundred men with him.

Those who came to David initially, his "mighty men," were people and families in distress, in debt, and discontented. They were in today's parlance, beat, broke and bitter. All too often, these are the first to heed the call of a leader with a new revelation. But they were committed to David and his purpose of bringing in a kingdom. He worked with those whom God provided, and it was they who carried him to the throne!

Here is another leadership principle: "You can always teach competence to committed people, but it is harder to teach commitment to already competent people."

A contrast to David could be Saul. Where David attracted the committed, but not the competent, who came to him of their own free will in their distress, Saul went about looking for competence. 1 Samuel 15:52 tells us: "Now there was fierce war with the Philistines all the days of Saul. And when Saul saw any strong man or any valiant man, he took him for himself." It was Saul who came to a bad end, largely because of his poor character and disobedience to God, but his ways of recruiting did not serve him well either and it was one of these very strong, valiant men, David, whom God placed on Saul's throne in the end.

Do not waste your time looking for competence! Spend it training committed people into competence. It is okay to be like Mary and say: "How can these things be, since I am a virgin?" Be willing to accept the answer: Luke 1:35 and 37 says,

> 35 The Holy Spirit will come upon you, and the power of the Highest will overshadow you; therefore, also, that Holy One who is to be born will be called the Son of God.

37 For with God nothing will be impossible."

This is precisely what you and I need to hear and believe. The Holy Spirit will do it in you and through you. This is the way to build the *Ekklesia* God has called you to build. You can rest assured that what you are building is what Jesus already promised to build when He said,

17 . . . Blessed are you, Simon Bar-Jonah, for flesh and blood has not revealed this to you, but My Father who is in heaven. 18 And I also say to you that you are Peter, and on this rock *I will build My church, and the gates of Hades shall not prevail against it.* 19 And I will give you the keys of the

kingdom of heaven, and whatever you bind on earth [h]will be bound in heaven, and whatever you loose on earth will be loosed in heaven (Matthew 16:17b-19 emphasis added).

Once you truly believe this, you will recognize the leaders among you. You will spot them with a shepherd's eye as they graze among the other sheep. Then, you will be able to raise them up into who they are in the Lord. Not into what you want them to be. But into whom God designed them to be.

Soon, you will release them into their God-given strengths and anointing. And you will rejoice to see them spread their own wings and serve God and His people with power and wisdom. Finally, you will resource them into greatness from the reservoir of your experience and earned wisdom and then you will "eat the fruit from the branches of their tree with thanksgiving and satisfaction." It doesn't get any better than this!

ABOUT THE AUTHOR

Dr. Ronald E. Cottle has been serving the body of Christ for more than six decades. He has extensive experience in teaching, pastoring, public speaking, education administration and both radio and television.

He has developed more than one hundred advanced courses of Christian development and biblical training and has authored more than four dozen books encompassing ministry, leadership, biblical studies, and church development.

Dr. Cottle's teaching style has been called "scholarship on fire" by those who have attended his lectures. His unique style always contains the compassion of a shepherd, the urgency of a prophet and the wisdom of a statesman.

His thoughts and counsel are straightforward, dynamic, and powerful. His teachings will help today's spiritual leaders and other sincere "thinking Christians" to discover the mystery and the majesty of the Bible.

Dr. Cottle has earned a Bachelor of Arts (A.B.) degree from Florida Southern College, Lakeland, Florida; a Master of Divinity (M.Div.) from Lutheran Theological Seminary, Columbia, South Carolina; and a Doctor of Philosophy (Ph.D.) in Religion from the University of Southern California, Los Angeles. He also earned a Master of Science in Education (M.S.Ed.) and a Doctor of Education (Ed.D.) from U.S.C.

DR. RONALD E. COTTLE

For more information about Dr. Ron Cottle and his numerous books and teachings, go to: www.roncottle.com.

THE COTTLE LIBRARY

Dr. Cottle has worked tirelessly in his home office for the past two decades compiling his five hundred notebooks, fifty plus college courses, fifty plus books, hundreds of sermon outlines, publications, articles, and newsletters. Dr. Cottle and Dr. Thomas Hale are cataloging everything into an online library.

The library contains digital files (PDF and Microsoft Word) available for download, streaming audio files and streaming video files.

Please visit the library at: www.cottlelibrary.com

Printed in Great Britain
by Amazon